Group Policy
Fast Start

Smart Brain Training Solutions

Thank you for purchasing *Group Policy Fast Start*! We hope you'll look for other *Fast Start* guides from Smart Brain Training Solutions.

Table of Contents

1. Group Policy Essentials

Anyone working with Windows computers can use Group Policy to simplify the application of common and repetitive tasks as well as unique tasks that are difficult to implement manually but can be easily automated. Group Policy includes both managed settings, referred to as *policy settings*, and unmanaged settings, referred to as *policy preferences*. *Group Policy* is in fact a collection of preferences and settings that can be applied to user and computer configurations.

Group Policy allows you to apply desired configuration preferences and settings in discrete sets. This means that you can configure user desktops to meet the specific preferences and requirements of your organization and control the configuration of every computer on your network.

One way to think of Group Policy is as a set of rules that you can apply throughout a Windows network. Group Policy settings enable you to control the configuration of Windows operating systems and their components. You can also use policy settings to configure computer and user scripts, folder redirection, computer security, software installation, and more.

Group Policy preferences enable you to configure, deploy, and manage operating system and application settings that you were not able to manage using earlier implementations of Group Policy, including data sources, mapped drives, environment variables, network shares, folder options, shortcuts, and more. In many cases, you'll find that using Group Policy preferences is a better approach than configuring these settings in Windows images or using logon scripts.

The key difference between preferences and policy settings is enforcement. Group Policy strictly enforces policy settings. You use policy settings to control the configuration of the operating system and its components. You also use policy settings to disable the user interface for settings that Group Policy is managing, which prevents users from changing those settings. Most policy settings are stored in policy-related branches of the registry. The operating system and compliant applications check the policy-related branches of the registry to determine whether and how various aspects of the operating system are controlled. Group Policy refreshes policy settings at a regular interval, which is every 90 to 120 minutes by default.

> **Note** When discussing whether applications support Group Policy, the terms *compliant application* and *Group Policy–aware application* are often used. A compliant or Group Policy–aware application is an application specifically written to support Group Policy. Whether an application is Group Policy–aware is extremely important. Group Policy–aware applications are programmed to check the policy-related branches of the registry to determine whether and how their features and various aspects of the operating system are controlled. Noncompliant, unaware applications are not programmed to perform these checks.

In contrast, Group Policy does not strictly enforce policy preferences. Group Policy does not store preferences in the policy-related branches of the registry. Instead, it writes preferences to the same locations in the registry that an application or operating system feature uses to store the setting. This allows Group Policy preferences to support applications and operating system features that aren't Group Policy–aware and also does not disable application or operating system features in the user interface to prevent their use. Because of this behavior, users can change settings that were configured using policy preferences. Finally, although Group Policy by default refreshes preferences using the same interval as Group Policy settings, you can prevent Group Policy from refreshing individual preferences by choosing to apply them only once.

When working with policy settings, keep the following in mind:

- Most policy settings are stored in policy-based areas of the registry.
- Settings are enforced.
- User interface options may be disabled.
- Settings are refreshed automatically.
- Settings require Group Policy–aware applications.
- Original settings are not changed.
- Removing the policy setting restores the original settings.

When working with policy preferences, keep the following in mind:

- Preferences are stored in the same registry locations as those used by the operating system and applications.
- Preferences are not enforced.
- User interface options are not disabled.
- Settings can be refreshed automatically or applied once.
- Supports non-Group Policy–aware applications.
- Original settings are overwritten.

- Removing the preference item does not restore the original setting.

> **Real World**   The way you use policy settings or policy
> preferences depends on whether you want to enforce the item. To
> configure an item without enforcing it, use policy preferences and
> then disable automatic refresh. To configure an item and enforce
> the specified configuration, use policy settings or configure
> preferences and then enable automatic refresh.

2. Understanding Group Policy Objects

Group Policy is so important to a successful Active Directory
implementation that most administrators think of it as a component of
Active Directory. This is mostly true—and it is okay to think of it this
way—but you don't necessarily need Active Directory to use Group
Policy. You can use Group Policy in both enterprise (domain) and local
(workgroup) environments.

Global Group Policy

For enterprise environments in which Active Directory is deployed, the
complete set of policy settings and policy preferences is available. This
policy set is referred to as *domain-based Group Policy*, *Active Directory–
based Group Policy*, or simply *Group Policy*. On domain controllers,
Group Policy is stored in the SYSVOL that Active Directory uses for
replicating policies.

Group Policy is represented logically as an object called a Group Policy object (GPO). A GPO is simply a collection of policy settings and preferences. Every GPO has a related Group Policy Container (GPC) and a related Group Policy Template (GPT).

The Group Policy Container for a GPO is stored in the Active Directory database and replicated through normal Active Directory replication. The GPC is used to store properties related to the GPO and is identified with a globally unique identifier (GUID).

The Group Policy Template (GPT) for a GPO is stored in the SYSVOL and replicated through SYSVOL replication. The GPT is used to store files related to the GPO on disk and is identified with the same GUID as the Group Policy Container.

Linking a GPO to components of the Active Directory structure is how you apply Group Policy. In your Active Directory structure, GPOs can be linked to:

- **Sites**   A *site* is a combination of one or more IP subnets connected by highly reliable links. You use sites to create a directory structure that mirrors the physical structure of your organization. A site typically has the same boundaries as your local area networks (LANs). Because site mappings are separate and independent from logical components in the directory, there's no necessary relationship between your network's physical structures and the logical structures in the directory.
- **Domains**   *A domain* is a logical grouping of objects that share a common directory database. In the directory, a domain is represented as a container object. Within a domain, you can create accounts for users, groups, and computers as well as for shared

resources such as printers and folders. Access to domain objects is controlled by security permissions.

- **Organizational units** An *organizational unit (OU)* is a logical container used to organize objects within a domain. Because an OU is the smallest scope to which you can delegate authority, you can use an OU to help manage administration of accounts for users, groups, and computers and for administration of other resources, such as printers and shared folders. By adding an OU to another OU, you can create a hierarchy within a domain. Because each domain has its own OU hierarchy, the OU hierarchy of a domain is independent from that of other domains.

You can create multiple GPOs, and by linking them to different locations in your Active Directory structure, you can apply the related settings to the users and computers in those Active Directory containers.

Because of the object-based hierarchy in Active Directory, the settings of top-level GPOs are applied to lower-level GPOs automatically by default. For example, a setting for the imaginedlands.com domain is applied to the Sales OU within that domain, and the domain settings will be applied to users and computers in the Sales OU. If you don't want policy settings to be applied, you may be able to override or block settings to ensure that only the GPO settings for the low-level GPOs are applied.

Note   With domain-based Group Policy, you might think that the forest or domain functional level would affect how Group Policy is used, but this is not the case. The forest and domain do not need to be in any particular functional mode to use Group Policy.

When you create a domain, two Active Directory GPOs are created automatically:

- **Default Domain Controllers Policy GPO**   A default GPO created for and linked to the Domain Controllers OU that is applicable to all domain controllers in a domain as long as they are members of this OU.
- **Default Domain Policy GPO**   A default GPO that is created for and linked to the domain within Active Directory.

You can create additional GPOs as necessary and link them to the sites, domains, and OUs you created. For example, you could create a GPO called Sales Policy and then link it to the Sales OU. The policy then applies to that OU.

Local Group Policy

For local environments, you can use a subset of Group Policy called *local Group Policy*. As the name implies, local Group Policy allows you to manage policy settings that affect everyone who logs on to the local machine. This means local Group Policy applies to any user or administrator who logs on to a computer that is a member of a workgroup, as well as to any user or administrator who logs on locally to a computer that is a member of a domain. Local Group Policy is stored locally on individual computers in the %SystemRoot%\System32\GroupPolicy folder.

Like Active Directory–based Group Policy, local Group Policy is managed through a GPO. This GPO is referred to as the Local Group Policy object (LGPO). On Windows Vista and later, which support multiple LGPOs, additional user-specific and group-specific LGPOs are stored in the %SystemRoot%\System32\GroupPolicyUsers folder.

Because local Group Policy is a subset of Group Policy, there are many things you can't do locally that you can do in a domain setting. First, you can't manage any policy preferences. Second, you can only manage a limited subset of policy settings. Generally speaking, the policy settings that you can't manage locally have to do with features that require Active Directory, such as software installation.

Beyond these fundamental differences between local Group Policy and Active Directory–based Group Policy, both types of policy are managed in much the same way. In fact, you use the same tools to manage both. The key difference is in the GPO you use. On a local machine, you work exclusively with the LGPOs. If you have deployed Active Directory, however, you can work with domain, site, and OU GPOs in addition to LGPOs.

All computers running Windows have LGPOs. The LGPOs are always processed. However, they have the least precedence, which means their settings can be superseded by site, domain, and OU settings. Although domain controllers have LGPOs, Group Policy for domain controllers is managed best through the Default Domain Controllers GPO.

> **Tip** Keep in mind that Group Policy is set within the directory itself. Settings are applied in this basic order: local, site, domain, and then OU. In the default configuration (where enforcement and blocking are not used), the last setting applied is the one in effect.

3. Managing Group Policy

Now that you know how GPOs are used, let's look at how you manage Group Policy. I discuss basic tools and techniques in this section as well as how to install additional tools you might need. You'll find in-depth discussions for working with Group Policy throughout the rest of the book.

Working with Group Policy

When you install Active Directory to configure your infrastructure, Active Directory creates default user accounts and groups to help you manage the directory and configure security. The default users and groups available include:

- **Administrator** A default user account with domainwide access and privileges. By default, the Administrator account for a domain is a member of these groups: Administrators, Domain Admins, Domain Users, Enterprise Admins, Group Policy Creator Owners, and Schema Admins.
- **Administrators** A local group that provides full administrative access to an individual computer or a single domain, depending on its location. Because this group has complete access, you should be very careful about adding users to it. To make someone an administrator for a local computer or domain, all you need to do is make that person a member of this group. Only members of the Administrators group can modify this account. Default members of this group include Administrator, Domain Admins, and Enterprise Admins.
- **Domain Admins** A global group designed to help you administer all the computers in a domain. Members of this group have

administrative control over all computers in a domain because they are members of the Administrators group by default. To make someone an administrator for a domain, make that person a member of this group.

- **Enterprise Admins** A global or universal group designed to help you administer all the computers in a domain tree or forest. Members of this group have administrative control over all computers in the enterprise because the group is a member of the Administrators group by default. To make someone an administrator for the enterprise, make that person a member of this group.

- **Group Policy Creator Owners** A global group designed to help you administer group policies. Members of this group have administrative control over Group Policy.

- **Schema Admins** A global group designed to help you administer Active Directory schema. Members of this group have administrative control over schema.

Whenever you work with Group Policy, be sure that you are using a user account that is a member of the appropriate group or groups.

Group Policy Administration Tools

You can manage Group Policy by using both graphical administration tools and command-line tools. The graphical tools are the easiest to work with, but if you master the command-line tools, you will often be able to accomplish tasks more quickly. When you use the command-line tools with the Task Scheduler, you might even be able to automate routine tasks.

> **Note** Appendix A, "Installing Group Policy Extensions and Tools," provides detailed instructions on installing additions and extensions for Group Policy. The appendix discusses:

1. Installing the Remote Server Administration Tools.

2. Installing Group Policy client-side extensions.

3. Installing the client and server components for Advanced Group Policy Management (AGPM).

Graphical Administration Tools

The graphical administration tools for working with Group Policy are provided as custom consoles as well as individual snap-ins for the Microsoft Management Console (MMC). You can access these tools directly on the Administrative Tools menu or add them to any updatable MMC. If you're using another computer with access to a Windows Server 2008 domain, the tools won't be available until you install them. One technique for installing these tools is to use the Add Feature Wizard.

You manage Active Directory–based Group Policy by using the Group Policy Management Console (GPMC), shown in Figure 1. You can add the GPMC to any installation of Windows Server 2008 by using the Add Features Wizard.

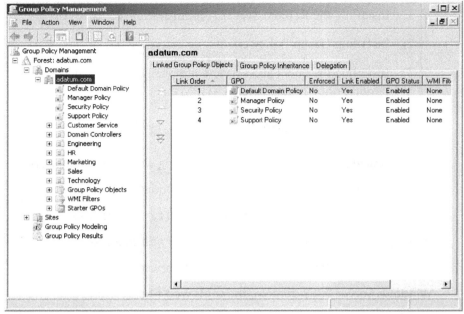

FIGURE 1 *Group Policy Management Console.*

Windows Server 2008 includes an updated version of the Group Policy
Management Console (GPMC). In this updated version, the Group Policy
preferences are built in. Additionally, you can configure preferences by
installing the Remote Server Administration Tools (RSAT) on a computer
running Windows Vista SP1 or later. For Windows Vista SP1 or later, the
version of GPMC included with RSAT is the updated version of GPMC.
After you add the GPMC to a computer running Windows Vista, it is
available on the Administrative Tools menu.

You use GPMC to perform these tasks:

- Create, edit, and delete GPOs
- Copy, import, and export GPOs
- Back up and restore GPOs

- Model GPOs prior to deployment to determine how their settings would affect users and computers
- Model existing GPOs to determine how their settings are affecting users and computers

When you want to edit a GPO in the GPMC, the GPMC opens the Group Policy Management Editor, shown in Figure 2. You use the editor to manage policy settings and preferences.

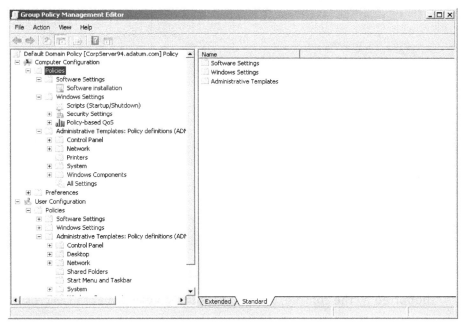

FIGURE 2 *Group Policy Management Editor.*

Also available are the Group Policy Starter GPO Editor and the Local Group Policy Editor. You use the Group Policy Starter GPO Editor to create and manage Starter Group Policy objects, which are meant to provide a starting point for new policy objects that you want to use throughout your organization. When you create a policy object, you can specify a starter GPO as the source or basis of the new object. You use the Local Group Policy Editor, shown in Figure 3, to create and manage policy objects for the local computer—as opposed to settings for an entire site, domain, or organizational unit.

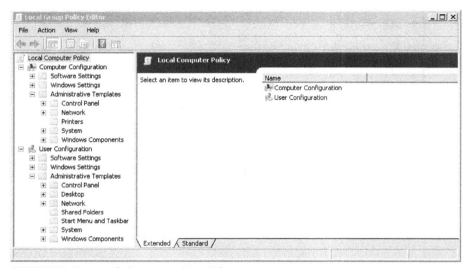

FIGURE 3 *Local Group Policy Editor.*

Command-Line Tools

GPMC provides a comprehensive set of Component Object Model (COM) interfaces that you can use to script many of the operations supported by the console. Samples scripts are available at the Microsoft Download Center Web site (*http://www.microsoft.com/downloads*). For the most recent version of the scripts, search the download site for "Group Policy Management Console Sample Scripts." Other command-line tools for working with Group Policy include:

- **ADPREP** Used to prepare a forest or domain for installation of domain controllers. To prepare a domain prior to installing Windows Server 2008 for the first time, you run *adprep*

/domainprep /gpprep on the server that holds the infrastructure operations master role.

- **GPFIXUP** Used to resolve domain name dependencies in Group Policy objects and Group Policy links after a domain rename operation.
- **GPRESULT** Used to see what policy is in effect and to troubleshoot policy problems.
- **GPUPDATE** Used to refresh Group Policy manually. If you enter **gpupdate** at a command prompt, both the Computer Configuration settings and the User Configuration settings in Group Policy are refreshed on the local computer.
- **LDIFDE** Used to import and export directory information. You'll use this tool to help you perform advanced backup and recovery of policy settings that are stored outside GPOs. Specifically, you can use this tool to back up and restore a large number of Windows Management Instrumentation (WMI) filters at one time (as discussed on the Group Policy team blog at *http://go.microsoft.com/fwlink/?linkid=109519*).
- **NETSH IPSEC** Used to view and manage a computer IP Security (IPSec) configuration. Use *netsh ipsec static show all* to display the static settings and policies for IPSec. Use *netsh ipsec dynamic show all* to display dynamic settings and policies for IPSec.

> **Real World** I include NETSH IPSEC in the list of important Group Policy tools because Group Policy backups created in the GPMC do not contain IPSec settings. These settings are backed up with system state backups. Because of this, you may want to track any IPSec settings and policies used, and NETSH IPSEC allows you to do this.

The Group Policy management tools provide access to Group Policy objects. There are several quick and easy ways to work with GPOs directly. At an elevated, administrator command line, you can open the computer's LGPO for editing in the Local Group Policy Editor by entering **gpedit**. To open another computer's LGPO, use the following syntax:

```
gpedit.msc /gpcomputer:"ComputerName"
```

where *ComputerName* is the host name or fully qualified domain name of the computer. The remote computer name must be enclosed in double quotation marks such as:

```
gpedit.msc /gpcomputer:"CorpServer82"
```

or

```
gpedit.msc
/gpcomputer:"CorpServer82.imaginedlands.com"
```

At an elevated, administrator command line, you can open a GPO for editing in the Group Policy Management Editor. The basic syntax is:

```
gpedit.msc /gpobject:"LDAP://CN=GPOID,
CN=Policies,CN=System,DC=DomainName,DC=com"
```

where *GPOID* is the unique identifier for the GPO as listed on the Details tab when a GPO is selected in the Group Policy Management Console, and *Domain Name* is the single part name of the domain in which you created the GPO. The entire object path must be enclosed in double quotation marks, such as:

```
gpedit.msc /gpobject:"LDAP://CN={6AC1786C-145d-
21E3-956D-00C04FB123D4},CN=Policies,CN=System,
DC=imaginedlands,DC=com"
```

In this example, the GPO being opened for editing is the GPO with the unique identifier {6AC1786C-145d-21E3-956D-00C04FB123D4} in the imaginedlands.com domain.

You can use an editor command that targets a specific GPO to quickly open a GPO that you commonly view or modify. If you save the command in a Shortcut on the desktop or the Start menu, you'll have a fast and easy way to access the GPO. In a Command Prompt window, you can copy an editor command you've entered by right-clicking within the Command Prompt window, and then clicking Mark. If you drag the mouse pointer over the command and then press Enter, you'll copy the command to the Windows clipboard. You can then create a desktop shortcut by right-clicking an open area of the desktop, pointing to New and then clicking Shortcut.

When the Create Shortcut wizard starts, press Ctrl+V to paste the copied command into the Type The Location Of The Item box, and then click Next. When prompted, enter a Name for the shortcut, such as Enhanced Security GPO, and then click Finish. Now, when you double-click the shortcut, you'll start the Group Policy Management Editor with your target GPO opened for viewing and editing.

4. Applying and Linking Group Policy Objects

Group Policy provides a convenient and effective way to manage both preferences and settings for computers and users. With Group Policy, you can manage preferences and settings for thousands of users or computers in the same way that you manage preferences and settings for one computer or user—and without ever leaving your desk. To do this, you use one of several management tools to change a preference or setting to the value you want, and this change is applied throughout the network to the subset of computers and users you target.

Previously, making many of the administrative changes that Group Policy enables was possible only by hacking the Windows registry, and each change had to be made individually on each target computer. With Group Policy, you can simply enable or disable a policy to tweak a registry value or other preference or setting, and the change will apply automatically the next time Group Policy is refreshed. Because changes can be modeled through the Group Policy Management Console before the modifications are applied, you can be certain of the effect of each desired change. Prior to deploying a change, you can save the state of Group Policy. If something goes wrong, you can restore Group Policy to its original state. When you restore the state of Group Policy, you can be certain that all changes are undone the next time Group Policy is refreshed.

Policy Sets Within GPOs

Before you deploy Group Policy for the first time or make changes to existing policy, you should ensure you have a thorough understanding of:

- How Group Policy has changed with the introduction of each new version of the Windows operating system.
- How you can update Group Policy to include the preferences and settings available in a new Windows operating system.
- How Group Policy is applied to a local computer as well as throughout an Active Directory environment.

- How default policy sets are used and when default policy applies.
- When to use policy preferences and when to use policy settings.

You store Group Policy preferences and settings in Group Policy objects (GPOs). Within Group Policy Objects, two distinct sets of policies are defined:

- **Computer policies** These apply to computers and are stored under Computer Configuration in a Group Policy object.
- **User policies** These apply to users and are stored under User Configuration in a Group Policy object.

Both Computer Configuration and User Configuration have Policies and Preferences nodes. You use:

- Computer Configuration\Policies to configure policy settings targeted to specific computers.
- Computer Configuration\Preferences to configure policy preferences targeted to specific computers.
- User Configuration\Policies to configure policy settings targeted to specific users.
- User Configuration\Preferences to configure policy preferences targeted to specific users.

Initial processing of the related policies is triggered by two unique events:

- **Processing of computer policies is triggered when a computer is started.** When a computer is started and the network connection is initialized, computer policies are applied.
- **Processing of user policies is triggered when a user logs on to a computer.** When a user logs on to a computer, user policies are applied.

Once applied, policies are automatically refreshed to keep settings current and to reflect any changes that might have been made. By default, Group Policy on domain controllers is refreshed every 5 minutes. For workstations and other types of servers, Group Policy is refreshed every 90 to 120 minutes by default. In addition, most security settings are refreshed every 16 hours regardless of whether any policy settings have changed in the intervening time. Other factors can affect Group Policy refreshes, including how slow-link detection is defined (per the Group Policy Slow Link Detection Policy under Computer Configuration\Policies\Administrative Templates\System\Group Policy) and policy processing settings for policies under Computer Configuration\Policies\Administrative Templates\System\Group Policy. You can check the last refresh of Group Policy using the Group Policy Management Console.

GPO Types

As discussed previously, there are two types of policy objects: Active Directory--based Group Policy objects (GPOs) and Local Group Policy objects (LGPOs).

Active Directory supports three levels of Group Policy objects:

- **Site GPOs**   Group Policy objects applied at the site level to a particular Active Directory site.
- **Domain GPOs**   Group Policy objects applied at the domain level to a particular Active Directory domain.
- **Organizational Unit (OU) GPOs**   Group Policy objects applied at the OU level to a particular Active Directory OU.

Through inheritance, a GPO applied to a parent container is inherited by a child container. This means that a policy preference or setting applied to a parent object is passed down to a child object. For example, if you apply a policy setting in a domain, the setting is inherited by organizational units within the domain. In this case, the GPO for the domain is the parent object and the GPOs for the organizational units are the child objects.

In an Active Directory environment, the basic order of inheritance goes from the site level to the domain level to the organizational unit level. This means that the Group Policy preferences and settings for a site are passed down to the domains within that site, and the preferences and settings for a domain are passed down to the organizational units within that domain.

> **Tip** As you might expect, you can override inheritance. To do this, you specifically assign a policy preference or setting for a child container that contradicts the policy preference or setting for the parent. As long as overriding the policy is allowed (that is, overriding isn't blocked), the child's policy preference or setting will be applied appropriately.

Windows Vista, Windows Server 2008, and later versions allow the use of multiple LGPOs on a single computer (as long as the computer is not a domain controller). On compliant computers, there are three layers of LGPOs:

- **Local Group Policy object** The Local Group Policy object is at the top of the policy hierarchy for the local computer. The LGPO is the only local computer policy object that allows both computer configuration and user configuration settings to be applied to all users of the computer.

- **Administrators Local Group Policy object / Non-Administrators Local Group Policy object**   Whether the Administrators Local Group Policy object or the Non-Administrators Local Group Policy object applies depends on the account being used. If the account is a member of the local computer's Administrator's group, the Administrators Group Policy object is applied. Otherwise, the Non-Administrators Group Policy object is applied. This object contains only user configuration settings.

- **User-specific Local Group Policy object**   A user-specific Local Group Policy object applies only to an individual user or to members of a particular group. This object contains only user configuration settings.

These layers of LGPOs are processed in the following order: Local Group Policy object, Administrators or Non-Administrators Local Group Policy object, and then user-specific Local Group Policy object.

Real World   When computers are being used in a stand-alone configuration rather than a domain configuration, you may find that multiple LGPOs are useful because you no longer have to explicitly disable or remove settings that interfere with your ability to manage a computer before performing administrator tasks. Instead, you can implement one local policy object for administrators and another local policy object for nonadministrators. In a domain configuration, however, you might not want to use multiple LGPOs. In domains, most computers and users already have multiple Group Policy objects applied to them—adding multiple LGPOs to this already varied mix can make managing Group Policy confusing. Therefore, you might want to disable processing of LGPOs, and you can do this through

> Group Policy. To disable processing of Local Group Policy objects on computers running Windows Vista, Windows Server 2008 or later, you must enable the Turn Off Local Group Policy Objects Processing setting in an Active Directory–based Group Policy object that the computer processes. When you are editing a GPO in the Group Policy Management Editor, this setting is located under Computer Configuration\Policies. Expand Administrative Templates\System\Group Policy, and then double-click the Turn Off Local Group Policy Objects Processing entry.

Putting this all together when both Active Directory and local policies are in place, policies are applied in the following order:

1. Local GPOs
2. Site GPOs
3. Domain GPOs
4. Organizational unit GPOs
5. Child organizational unit GPOs

Because the available preferences and settings are the same for all policy objects, a preference or setting in one policy object can possibly conflict with a preference or setting in another policy object. Compliant operating systems resolve conflicts by overwriting any previous preference or setting with the last read and most current preference or setting. Therefore, the final preference or setting written is the one that Windows uses. For example, by default, organizational unit policies have precedence over domain policies. As you might expect, there are exceptions to the precedence rule.

GPO Links

In Active Directory, each site, domain, or OU can have one or more GPOs associated with it. The association between a GPO and a site, domain, or OU is referred to as a *link*. For example, if a GPO is associated with a domain, the GPO is said to be linked to that domain.

GPOs are stored in a container called Group Policy Objects. This container is replicated to all domain controllers in a domain, so by default all GPOs are also replicated to all domain controllers in a domain. The link (association) between a domain, site, or OU is what makes a GPO active and applicable to that domain, site, or OU.

Linking can be applied in two ways:

- You can link a GPO to a specific site, domain, or OU. For example, if a GPO is linked to a domain, the GPO applies to users and computers in that domain. The main reason for linking a GPO to a specific site, domain, or OU is to keep with the normal rules of inheritance.
- You can link a GPO to multiple levels in Active Directory. For example, a single GPO could be linked to a site, a domain, and multiple OUs. In this case, the GPO applies to each of these levels within Active Directory. The main reason for linking a GPO to multiple levels within Active Directory is to create direct associations between a GPO and multiple sites, domains, and OUs irrespective of how inheritance would normally apply.

You can also unlink a GPO from a site, domain, or OU. This removes the direct association between the GPO and the level within Active Directory from which you've removed the link. For example, if a GPO is linked to a site called First Seattle Site and also to the imaginedlands.com domain, you can remove the link from the imaginedlands.com domain, removing the association between the GPO and the domain. The GPO is then linked only to the site. If you later remove the link between the site and the GPO, the GPO is completely unlinked. A GPO that has been unlinked from all levels within Active Directory still exists within the Group Policy Objects container, but it is inactive.

Connecting to and Working with GPOs

When you use the GPMC to work with GPOs, by default the corresponding changes are made on the domain controller that is acting as the PDC emulator. In this way, the PDC emulator is the central point of contact for GPO creation, modification, and deletion. Active Directory manages policy in this way to ensure that changes to the GPO structure can be implemented only on a single authoritative domain controller and that only one administrator at a time is granted access to a particular GPO. Because the PDC emulator role is specified at the domain level, there is only one PDC emulator in a domain, and therefore only one place where policy settings are changed by default. If the PDC emulator is unavailable when you are trying to work with policy settings, you get a prompt that enables you to work with policy settings on the domain controller to which you are connected or on any available domain controller.

Any user who is a member of the Domain Admins or Enterprise Admins group can view and work with Active Directory–based Group Policy. Unlike local Group Policy, GPO creation and linking are separate operations with Active Directory–based Group Policy. First you create a GPO and define a group of policy settings to achieve desired results. Then you apply your GPO and make it "live" by linking it to the container or containers within Active Directory where it will be applied.

Although creating and linking GPOs are two distinct operations, the GPMC does allow you to create GPOs and simultaneously link them to a domain or OU within the directory. This means you have two options for creating and linking GPOs. You can:

- Create a GPO and then later link it to a domain or OU within the directory.
- Create a GPO and simultaneously link it to a domain or OU within the directory.

To link a GPO to a site, the GPO must already exist.

The link is what tells Active Directory to apply the preferences and settings specified in the GPO. For example, you can create a GPO called Main Imaginedlands.com Domain Policy and then link it to the Domain container for imaginedlands.com. According to the default (standard) inheritance and policy processing rules, once you link a GPO to a container, the related policy preferences and settings are applied to that container, and lower-level containers within the directory can also inherit the preferences settings. This means a linked GPO can affect every user and computer throughout the enterprise—or some subset of users and computers throughout the enterprise.

5. Using Default Policies

With Windows Server, you create a domain by establishing the first domain controller for that domain. This typically means logging on to a stand-alone server as a local administrator, running the Domain Controller Installation Wizard (DCPROMO), and then specifying that you want to establish a new forest or domain. When you establish the domain and the domain controller, two GPOs are created by default:

- **Default Domain Policy GPO**   A GPO created for and linked to the domain within Active Directory. This GPO is used to establish baselines for a selection of policy settings that apply to all users and computers in a domain.
- **Default Domain Controllers Policy GPO**   A GPO created for and linked to the Domain Controllers OU that is applicable to all domain controllers in a domain (as long as they aren't moved from this OU). This GPO is used to manage security settings for domain controllers in a domain.

These default GPOs are essential to the proper operation and processing of Group Policy. By default, the Default Domain Controllers Policy GPO has the highest precedence among GPOs linked to the Domain Controllers OU, and the Default Domain Policy GPO has the highest precedence among GPOs linked to the domain. As you'll learn in the sections that follow, the purpose and use of each default GPO is a bit different.

> **Note**   The default GPOs are used to establish defaults for a limited subset of policy settings. Neither default GPO is used to establish default preferences.

Working with the Default Domain Policy GPO

The Default Domain Policy GPO is a complete policy set that includes settings for managing any area of policy, but it isn't meant for general management of Group Policy. As a best practice, you should edit the Default Domain Policy GPO only to manage the default Account policies settings and three specific areas of Account policies:

- **Password policy** Determines default password policies for domain controllers, such as password history and minimum password length settings.
- **Account lockout policy** Determines default account lockout policies for domain controllers, such as account lockout duration and account lockout threshold.
- **Kerberos policy** Determines default Kerberos policies for domain controllers, such as maximum tolerance for computer clock synchronization.

To manage other areas of policy, you should create a new GPO and link it to the domain or an appropriate OU within the domain. That said, several policy settings are exceptions to the rule that the Default Domain Policy GPO (or the highest precedence GPO linked to the domain) is used only to manage Account policies. These policies (located in the Group Policy Management Editor under Computer Configuration\Policies\Windows Settings\Security Settings\Local Policies\Security Options) are as follows:

- **Accounts: Rename Administrator Account** Renames the built-in Administrator account on all computers throughout the domain, setting a new name for the account so that it is better protected from malicious users. Note that this policy affects the logon name of the account, not the display name. The display name remains Administrator or whatever you set it to. If an administrator changes the logon name for this account through Active Directory Users And Computers, it automatically reverts to what is specified in this policy setting the next time Group Policy is refreshed.

- **Accounts: Administrator Account Status**   Forcibly disables the built-in Administrator account on all computers throughout the domain. If you disable the Administrator account, keep in mind that this account is always available when you boot a computer in safe mode.

- **Accounts: Guest Account Status**   Forcibly disables the built-in Guest account on all computers throughout the domain. If you disable the Guest account, keep in mind that network logons will fail if you set the security option Network Access: Sharing And Security Model For Local Accounts to Guest Only.

- **Accounts: Rename Guest Account**   Renames the built-in Guest account on all computers throughout the domain, setting a new name for the built-in Guest account so that it is better protected from malicious users. Note that this policy affects the logon name of the account, not the display name. The display name remains Guest or whatever else you set it to. If an administrator changes the logon name for this account through Active Directory Users And Computers, it automatically reverts to what is specified in this policy setting the next time Group Policy is refreshed.

- **Network Security: Force Logoff When Logon Hours Expire**   Forces users to log off from the domain when logon hours expire. For example, if you set the logon hours as 8 A.M. to 6 P.M. for the user, the user is forced to log off at 6 P.M.

- **Network Security: Do Not Store LAN Manager Hash Value On Next Password Change**   Determines whether at the next password change the LAN Manager hash value for the new password is stored. Because this value is stored locally in the security database, a password could be compromised if the security database was attacked. On Windows Vista, Windows Server 2008 and later, this setting is typically enabled by default.

- **Network Access: Allow Anonymous SID/Name Translation** Determines whether an anonymous user can request security identifier (SID) attributes for another user. If this setting is enabled, a malicious user could use the well-known Administrators SID to obtain the real name of the built-in Administrator account, even if the account has been renamed. If this setting is disabled, computers and applications running in legacy Windows domains may not be able to communicate with Windows Server 2003 and later domains.

Additionally, certificates stored as policy settings for data recovery agents in the domain are also exceptions. These policies are stored under Computer Configuration\Policies\Windows Settings\Security Settings\Public Key Policies\Encrypting File System). You typically manage these policy settings through the GPO that is linked to the domain level and has the highest precedence. As with Account policies, this is the Default Domain Policy GPO by default.

Wondering why configuring policy in this way is a recommended best practice? Well, if Group Policy becomes corrupted and stops working, you can use the Dcgpofix tool to restore the Default Domain Policy GPO to its original state (which would mean that you would lose all the customized settings you've applied to this GPO). Further, some policy settings can only be configured at the domain level, and configuring them in the Default Domain Policy GPO (or the highest precedence GPO linked to the domain) makes the most sense.

> **Note**   Bottom line, if you define Account policies in multiple GPOs linked to a domain, the settings will be merged according to the link order of these GPOs. The GPO with a link order of 1 will always have the highest precedence.

You can access the Default Domain Policy GPO in several ways. If you are using the GPMC, you'll see the Default Domain Policy GPO when you click the domain name in the console tree, as shown in Figure 4. Right-click the Default Domain Policy node and select Edit to get full access to the Default Domain Policy GPO.

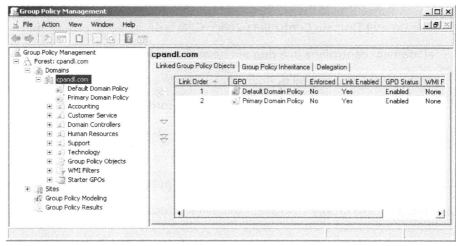

FIGURE 4 *Accessing the Default Domain Policy GPO in GPMC.*

In the Group Policy Management Editor, under Computer Configuration, expand Policies\Windows Settings\Security Settings\Local Policies as shown in Figure 5. You can then work with Audit Policy, User Rights Assignment, and Security Options as necessary.

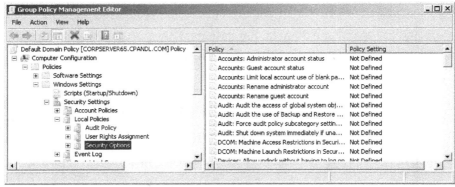

FIGURE 5 *Editing the Default Domain Policy GPO.*

Working with the Default Domain Controllers Policy GPO

The Default Domain Controllers Policy GPO is designed to ensure that all domain controllers in a domain have the same security settings. This is important because all domain controllers in an Active Directory domain are equal. If they were to have different security settings, they might behave differently, and this would be counter to the way Active Directory is designed to work. If one domain controller has a specific policy setting, this policy setting should be applied to all domain controllers to ensure consistent behavior across a domain.

The Default Domain Controllers Policy GPO is linked to the Domain Controllers OU. This ensures that it is applicable to all domain controllers in a domain as long as they aren't moved from this OU. Because all domain controllers are placed in the Domain Controllers OU by default, any security setting changes you make will apply to all domain controllers by default. The key security areas that you should manage consistently include:

- **Audit policy** Determines default auditing policies for domain controllers.
- **User rights assignment** Determines default user rights assignment for domain controllers.
- **Security options** Determines default security options for domain controllers.

Microsoft recommends that you not make any other changes to the Default Domain Controllers Policy GPO. Keep in mind that this GPO applies only to domain controllers because it is linked to the Domain Controllers OU and all domain controllers are members of this OU by default.

Moving a domain controller out of the Domain Controllers OU can adversely affect domain management and can also lead to inconsistent behavior during logon and authentication. Why? When you move a domain controller out of the Domain Controllers OU, the Default Domain Controllers Policy GPO no longer applies unless you've linked this GPO to the destination OU. Further, any GPO linked to the destination OU is applied to the domain controller.

Therefore, if you move a domain controller out of the Domain Controllers OU, you should carefully manage its security settings thereafter. For example, if you make security changes to the Default Domain Controllers Policy GPO, you should ensure that those security changes are applied to domain controllers stored in OUs other than the Domain Controllers OU.

You can access the Default Domain Controllers Policy GPO in several ways. If you are using the GPMC, you'll see the Default Domain

Controllers Policy GPO when you click the Domain Controllers node in the console tree. Then right-click the Default Domain Controllers Policy and select Edit to get full access to the Default Domain Controllers Policy GPO.

> **Real World** Microsoft product support does not support moving a domain controller out of the Domain Controllers OU. If you've done so and are having problems with your domain controllers that could be related to this action, Microsoft product support will ask you to move the domain controller back to the Domain Controllers OU.
>
> Other components and products rely on the Default Domain Controllers Policy GPO being present and linked in the domain. For example, Exchange Server may generate error events stating it cannot find a global catalog. Often, this occurs because you do not have the Default Domain Controllers Policy linked to the Domain Controllers OU or because you have moved domain controllers out of the Domain Controllers OU.

6. Using Policy Preferences and Settings

So far we've discussed how Group Policy has changed, how you can update policy, and how policy is applied, but I haven't discussed the specific ways in which you can use preferences and settings to help you better manage your network. I'll remedy that now by detailing uses for both preferences and settings. Because some overlap occurs in management areas for preferences and settings, I'll also discuss whether using settings or preferences is better suited to a particular task.

Using Policy Settings for Administration

A policy setting is a managed setting that you apply to control configuration, such as to restrict access to the Run dialog box. Most policy settings have three basic states:

- **Enabled**   The policy setting is turned on, and its settings are active. You typically enable a policy setting to ensure that it is enforced. Once enabled, some policy settings allow you to configure additional options that fine-tune how the policy setting is applied.
- **Disabled**   The policy setting is turned off, and its settings are not applied. Typically, you disable a policy setting to ensure that it is not enforced.
- **Not Configured**   The policy setting is not being used. No settings for the policy are either active or inactive and no changes are made to the configuration settings targeted by the policy.

By themselves, these states are fairly straightforward. However, these basic states can be affected by inheritance and blocking. That said, with the following two rules about inheritance and blocking in mind, you'll be well on your way to success with Group Policy:

- If inherited policy settings are strictly enforced, you cannot override them. This means the inherited policy setting is applied regardless of the policy state set in the current GPO.
- If inherited policy settings are blocked in the current GPO and not strictly enforced, the inherited policy setting is overridden. This means the inherited policy setting does not apply, and only the policy setting from the current GPO is applied.

Now that you know exactly how to apply individual policy settings, let's look at the administrative areas to which you can apply Group Policy. Through a special set of policies called Administrative Templates, you can manage just about every aspect of the Windows graphical user interface (GUI), from menus to the desktop, the taskbar, and more. The Administrative Template policy settings affect actual registry settings, so the available policies are nearly identical whether you are working with local Group Policy or domain-based Group Policy. You can use administrative templates to manage:

- **Control Panel** Controls access to and the options of Control Panel. You can also configure settings for Add Or Remove Programs, Display, Printers, and Regional And Language Options.
- **Desktop** Configures the Windows desktop, the availability and configuration of Active Desktop, and Active Directory search options from the desktop.
- **Network** Configures networking and network client options, including offline files, DNS clients, and network connections.
- **Printers** Configures printer publishing, browsing, spooling, and directory options.
- **Shared folders** Allows publishing of shared folders and Distributed File System (DFS) roots.
- **Start menu and taskbar** Configures the Start menu and taskbar, primarily by removing or hiding items and options.
- **System** Configures policies related to general system settings, disk quotas, user profiles, logon, power management, system restore, error reporting, and more.
- **Windows components** Configures whether and how to use various Windows components, such as Event Viewer, Task Scheduler, and Windows Updates.

Real World   You can obtain additional administrative templates for Microsoft Office at the Microsoft Download Center (*http://download.microsoft.com*). At the Download Center, click Home & Office under Download Categories. Search the Home & Office category for "Office customization tool," and then click the link for the most recent release. Next, download and run the self-extracting executable. When prompted, accept the license terms and then click Continue. You will then be able to select a destination folder for the related files. Review the files you've just extracted.

To use the administrative templates in GPMC on your computer, copy the ADMX files to the %SystemRoot%\PolicyDefinitions folder and the ADML files to the appropriate language-specific subfolder of the PolicyDefinitions folder. Otherwise, to make the administrative templates available throughout the domain, copy the ADMX and ADML files to the appropriate folders within the SYSVOL on a domain controller.

Table 1 provides a list of administrative areas you can manage using Group Policy. Whether you are working with local Group Policy or Active Directory–based Group Policy, the areas of administration are similar. However, you can do much more with Active Directory–based Group Policy primarily because you cannot use local Group Policy to manage any features that require Active Directory.

TABLE 1 Key Administrative Areas That Can Be Managed with Policy Settings

Device/Drive installation	Controls the way device and driver installation works.
Device Installation restriction	Restricts the devices that can be deployed and used.
Disk quotas	Configures the way disk quotas are used and whether quotas are enforced, logged, or both.
Encrypted data recovery agents	Configures data recovery agents and their related certificates for use with the Encrypting File System (EFS).
File and folder security	Configures security permissions for files and folders.
Folder redirection	Moves critical data folders for users to network shares where they can be better managed and backed up regularly (domain-based Group Policy only).
General computer security	Establishes security settings for accounts, event logs, restricted groups, system services, the registry, and file systems. (With local Group Policy, you can only manage general computer security for account policies.)
Internet settings	Controls the ways Windows Internet Explorer can be used and establishes lockdown settings.
Internet Explorer maintenance	Configures the browser interface, security, important URLs, default programs, proxies, and more.
IP security	Configures IP security policy for clients, servers, and secure servers.
Local security policies	Configures policy for auditing, user rights assignment, and user privileges.
Offline files	Determines whether and how offline files are used.

Policy-based Quality of Service (QoS)	Manages network traffic to help improve quality of service for critical applications.
Power options	Configure power management plans and settings for devices. (Windows Vista or later)
Printer deployment	Configures printers for use. (Windows Vista or later)
Public key security	Configures public key policies for autoenrollment, EFS, enterprise trusts, and more.
Registry security	Configures security permissions for registry keys.
Restricted groups	Controls the membership of both Active Directory–based groups and local computer groups.
Scripts	Configures logon/logoff scripts for users and startup/shutdown scripts for computers.
Software installation	Configures automated deployment of new software and software upgrades (domain-based Group Policy only).
Software restriction	Restricts the software that can be deployed and used. Local Group Policy does not support user-based software restriction policies, only computer-based software restriction policies.
Start menu	Defines the available options on and the behavior of the Start menu.
System services	Configures startup state and security permissions for system services.
Wired networking (IEEE 802.3)	Configures wired network policies for authentication methods and modes that apply to wired clients (domain-based Group Policy only). Can also be used to validate server certificates, enable quarantine checks, enforce advanced 802.1X settings, and enable single sign on.

Wireless networking (IEEE 802.11)	Configures wireless network policies for access points, wireless clients, and preferred networks (domain-based Group Policy only). Can also be used to define permitted types of connections and block disallowed types of connections.

Using Policy Preference for Administration

A policy preference is an unmanaged setting that you apply to preconfigure an option for a user, such as to map a network share to a drive. Most policy preferences can be established using one of four different actions:

- **Create**   Creates the preference only if a preference does not already exist.
- **Replace**   Deletes the preference if it exists and then creates it, or creates the preference if it doesn't yet exist.
- **Update**   Modifies the preference if it exists. Otherwise, creates the preference.
- **Delete**   Deletes the preference if it exists.

As with states for policy settings, these actions are fairly straightforward. However, these basic actions also can be affected by inheritance and blocking. To help you navigate inheritance and blocking, keep these basic rules in mind:

- If inherited policy preferences are strictly enforced, you cannot override them. This means the inherited policy preference is applied regardless of the action defined in the current GPO.
- If inherited policy preferences are blocked in the current GPO and not strictly enforced, the inherited policy preference is overridden.

This means the inherited policy preference does not apply, and only the policy preference from the current GPO is applied.

Unlike policy settings, policy preferences apply only to Active Directory–based Group Policy. When you are working with Active Directory–based Group Policy, you can use policy preferences to configure the items discussed in Table 2.

TABLE 2 Key Elements That Can Be Configured with Policy Preferences

Applications	Application settings. Available when you install preference settings for an application.
Data Sources	Open Database Connectivity (ODBC) data sources
Devices	System devices, including USB ports, floppy drives, and removable media
Drive Maps	Network shares mapped to drive letters.
Environment	System and user environment variables
Files	Files that can be copied from a source location to a destination location.
Ini Files	Property values within .ini files.
Folders	Folders in a particular location on the file system.
Local Users And Groups	User and group accounts for the local computer.
Network Options	Virtual Private Networking and Dial-up Networking connections
Network shares	Shares, hidden shares, and administrative shares.
Printers	Printer configuration and mapping
Registry	Registry keys and values.

Scheduled Tasks	Scheduled tasks for automation
Services	System services
Shortcuts	Shortcuts for file system objects, URLs, or shell objects.

Through special preferences for Control Panel, you can also manage various aspects of the Windows graphical user interface (GUI). You can use these special preferences to manage:

- Folder settings as if you were using the options available in the Folder Options utility in Control Panel. Located in Computer | User Configuration\Preferences\Control Panel Settings\Folder Options.
- Internet settings as if you are using the options available in the Internet Options utility in Control Panel. Located in User Configuration\Preferences\Control Panel Settings\Internet Settings.
- Power schemes and power management options as if you were using the related utilities in Control Panel. Located in Computer | User Configuration\Preferences\Control Panel Settings\Power Options. (Windows XP only.)
- Regional and language settings as if you were using the options available in the Regional And Languages utility in Control Panel. Located in User Configuration\Preferences\Control Panel Settings\Regional Options.
- Start menu as if you were using the Start Menu Properties dialog box. Located in User Configuration\Preferences\Control Panel Settings\Start Menu.

Choosing Between Preferences and Settings

Because some management areas overlap between policy preferences and policy settings, you can sometimes perform a particular task in more than one way. For example, using policy settings, you can identify logon scripts that should be used. Within these scripts, you can map network drives, configure printers, create shortcuts, copy files and folders, and perform other tasks. Using policy preferences however, you could perform these same tasks without the need of using logon scripts. So which one should you use? Well, the truth is that there really isn't one right answer. It depends on what you want to do. In the following sections, I describe some general guidelines for specific areas of overlap.

> **Real World**   When a conflict occurs between a policy setting and a policy preference defined in a particular GPO, a registry-based policy setting will normally win. For conflicts between non-registry-based policy settings and preferences, the last value written wins (as determined by the order in which the client-side extensions for policy settings and preferences are processed). Determining whether a policy setting is registry-based or not is easy. All registry-based policy settings are defined in administrative templates.

Controlling Device Installation

Through policy settings, you can control device installation and enforce specific restrictions. The goal is to prevent users from installing specific types of hardware devices. You can specify that certain approved devices can be installed (according to the hardware ID of the device). You can also prevent installation of specific disapproved devices (again according to the hardware ID of the device). These policy settings only apply to Windows Vista, Windows Server 2008 or later and are found under Computer Configuration\Policies\Administrative Templates\System\Device Installation\Device Installation Restrictions.

While restrictions block the installation of a new device or prevent a device from being plugged back in after it has been unplugged, it doesn't prevent existing devices from being used. Why? The device drivers are already installed and the devices are already available, and because the device or drive isn't rechecked, it continues to work.

Using policy preferences, you can disable device classes, individual devices, port classes, and individual ports, but you cannot prevent a driver from loading. You disable devices by selecting a device class or device already installed on your management computer. You disable ports by selecting a port class or specific port already in use on your management computer. The related preferences are found under Computer | User Configuration\Preferences\Control Panel Settings\Devices.

While you can disable devices and ports using preferences, this doesn't prevent device drivers from installing. It also doesn't prevent a user with appropriate rights from enabling ports or devices in Device Manager. However, as Group Policy by default refreshes policy preferences using the same refresh interval as for policy settings, the preference would be reapplied during the next refresh interval. Therefore, unless you specifically elect to apply the preference once and not reapply it, the preference would be reapplied every 90 to 120 minutes.

Given how these technologies work, the best solution for your environment may depend on your goal. If you want to completely lock things down and prevent specific devices from being installed and used, you may want to use both policy settings and policy preferences to do the job. Policy settings could prevent specific devices from being installed, providing they weren't already installed. Policy preferences could disable devices already installed, providing that you've already installed the device on your management computer so it can be selected.

As a final thought, it is important to point out that the related policy settings apply only to Windows Vista, Windows Server 2008 or later, while the related policy preferences apply to any computer on which the client-side extensions for Group Policy Preferences are installed.

Controlling Files and Folders

Through policy settings, you can specify security permissions for files and folders. The goal is to establish specific access control lists (ACLs) for important files and folders. However, the files and folders must already exist on the target computers so that the ACLs can be applied. These policy settings apply to any computer that supports Group Policy and are found under Computer Configuration\Policies\Windows Settings\Security Settings\File System.

Using policy preferences, you can manage files and folders. Preferences for files work differently than preferences for folders. With files, you can create, update, or replace a file on a target computer by copying it from a source computer. You can also delete a file on a target computer. With folders, you can create, update, replace, or delete a folder in a specific location on a target computer. You can also specify whether to delete existing files and subfolders during the create, update, replace, or delete operation.

File and folder preferences apply to any computer on which the client-side extensions for Group Policy Preferences are installed. For files, the related preferences are found under Computer | User Configuration\Preferences\Windows Settings\Files. For folders, the related preferences are found under Computer | User Configuration\Preferences\Windows Settings\Folders.

Tip Group Policy also provides preferences for working with .ini files and shortcuts. Preferences for .ini files are limited to modifying values for designated properties within a specific section of the .ini file. Shortcut preferences are used to create shortcuts to files, folders, URLs, and shell objects in a specific location, such as the desktop.

Here, using policy settings and preferences together gives you the best of both worlds. Through preferences you have an easy way to copy files from a source computer to target computers and to manage folders. Through settings you have an easy way to apply desired security settings. Additionally, with files and folders, you might want to apply preferences only once and not reapply them. Otherwise, the create, update, replace, or delete operations will be reapplied during Group Policy refresh.

Controlling Internet Explorer

Group Policy offers a wide array of settings and preferences for Internet Explorer. There are so many options that even a few experts are confused as to what does what. The key things to focus on are the following:

- Policy settings under Computer Configuration\Policies\Administrative Templates\Windows Components\Internet Explorer are primarily meant to control Internet Explorer behavior. These settings configure browser security enhancements and help to lockdown Internet security zones.
- Policy settings under User Configuration\Policies\Windows Settings\Internet Explorer Maintenance are used to specify important URLs, such as those for home pages, search, support, favorites, and links. These settings are also used to customize the browser interface by adding custom logos, titles, and buttons to Internet Explorer and to establish default programs, proxies, and more.
- Preference settings under User Configuration\Preferences\Control Panel Settings\Internet Settings allow you to configure any of the options available in the Internet Options utility in Control Panel (which essentially includes every user-configurable option).

Because policy settings are managed and policy preferences are unmanaged, you can use policy settings when you want to enforce specific settings for Internet Explorer. Although you can configure Internet Explorer with preferences, the preferences are not enforced and users can change settings. That said, if you apply the preferences so that they are refreshed automatically as part of normal Group Policy refreshes, settings users change may be overwritten by your preferences.

When you want to customize the interface, the settings under Internet Explorer Maintenance are the ones you'll use. These settings allow you to configure home page URLs, search URLs, support URLs, favorites, and links. They also allow you to add custom logos, titles, and buttons.

Controlling Power Options

When you want to control power management settings, the choice between policy settings and policy preferences is easy. You use policy settings for Windows Vista, Windows Server 2008 or later.

Policy settings for Windows Vista, Windows Server 2008 or later are found under Computer | User Configuration\Policies\Administrative Templates\System\Power Management.

Controlling Printers

With policy settings, you can deploy printers to computers running any version of Windows that supports Group Policy. This technology establishes a connection to an existing shared printer.

To deploy printers to computers running Windows Vista, Windows Server 2008 or later, you can use policy settings under User Configuration\Policies\Windows Settings\Deployed Printers. To deploy printers to computers running earlier versions of Windows, you can push a printer connection to the computer using PushPrinterConnection.exe as a logon or startup script.

With policy preferences, you can map and configure printers. These preferences include options for configuring local printers as well as for mapping both TCP/IP and shared network printers. These policy preferences apply to any computer on which the client-side extensions for Group Policy Preferences are installed.

As printer preferences are much more versatile than printer settings, you'll probably want to use preferences to deploy printers. That said, if you've already configured printers to be deployed using policy settings, you don't need to switch to policy preferences and redeploy the printers.

Controlling Registry Keys and Values

Through policy settings, you can specify security permissions for registry keys. The goal is to establish specific access control lists (ACLs) for important registry keys. However, the registry keys must already exist on the target computers so that the ACLs can be applied. These policy settings apply to any computer that supports Group Policy and are found under Computer Configuration\Policies\Windows Settings\Security Settings\Registry.

Using policy preferences, you can create, update, replace, or delete registry keys. The related preferences are found under Computer | User Configuration\Preferences\Windows Settings\Registry. Although you can modify just about any registry key, it is contradictory to widely manage registry values through preferences. Why? Policy settings defined within the administrative templates set registry values for you so that you don't have to modify the registry directly. You can install additional administrative templates to manage the registry settings of other applications. If administrative templates aren't available for a particular application, you can create your own custom administrative template to manage the registry settings for the application.

Because of the conflicting goals, I recommend using policy preferences to manage individual registry keys and only in a limited number of situations. When you need to work with multiple or many registry keys, you should use preexisting administrative templates or consider creating your own custom administrative templates. Additionally, with registry keys, you might want to apply preferences only once and not reapply them. Otherwise, the create, update, replace, or delete operation will be reapplied during Group Policy refresh.

Controlling the Start Menu

When it comes to the Start menu, there is a lot of overlap between what you can configure with policy settings and what you can configure with policy preferences. With this in mind, you use policy settings and policy preferences to work with the Start menu in very different ways.

Through policy settings, you can control the options available on the Start menu and define the behavior of various Start menu options. With over 70 settings to choose from under User Configuration\Policies\Administrative Templates\Start Menu And Taskbar, there are many possibilities. You can specify that you want to clear the history of recently opened documents when a user logs off or that drag and drop is disabled on the Start menu. You can lock the taskbar, remove system tray icons, and turn off notifications.

Policy preferences for working with the Start menu are located in User Configuration\Preferences\Control Panel Settings\Start Menu. With policy preferences, you manage the options and behavior of the Start menu as if you were using the Start Menu Properties dialog box. You can configure both the standard Start menu and the classic Start menu. There are, however, no options for configuring the taskbar.

Controlling System Services

When you want to control system services, the choice between policy settings and policy preferences is easy. You can use policy settings to:

- Configure the service startup mode
- Specify the access permissions for services (which control who can start, stop, and pause the service)

Policy settings for services are locatd under Computer Configuration\Policies\Windows Settings\Security Settings\System Services.

You can use policy preferences to:

- Configure the service startup mode
- Configure a service action that can be used to start a stopped service, stop a started service, or stop and restart a service
- Specify the account under which the service runs and set the password for this account
- Specify recovery actions that determine how the service responds to failure

Policy preferences for services are located under Computer Configuration\Preferences\Control Panel Settings\Services.

Because policy settings are managed and policy preferences are unmanaged, you can use policy settings when you want to enforce specific startup modes and access permissions. Although you can configure services with preferences, the preferences are not enforced and users can change settings. If you apply the preferences so that they are refreshed, settings users change may be overwritten by your preferences.

Controlling Users and Groups

When you want to control users and groups, the choice between policy settings and policy preferences is easy. You use policy settings when you want to restrict the membership of either a group defined in Active Directory or a group on the local computer. You do this by specifying the members of the group and the groups of which the group is a member. The related policy settings are found in Computer | User Configuration\Policies\Windows Settings\Security Settings\Restricted Groups.

You use policy preferences to create, replace, update, or delete users and groups on the local computer. With local user accounts, you can also:

- Rename existing user accounts
- Set user account passwords
- Set status flags for user accounts

Status flags can be used to require users to change passwords at next log on, disable the account, or set an expiration date.

With local groups, you can also:

- Rename existing groups
- Add or remove the current user as a member
- Delete member users, member groups, or both

Policy preferences for local users and groups are located under Computer | User Configuration\Preferences\Control Panel Settings\Local Users And Groups.

Active
Directory

Fast
Start

A Quick Start Guide for Active Directory.

Smart Brain
Training Solutions

Exchange Online

A Quick Start Guide for Exchange Online, Office 365 and Windows Azure!

Smart Brain
Training Solutions

XML

Fast Start

Smart Brain
Training Solutions

www.ingramcontent.com/pod-product-compliance
Lightning Source LLC
Chambersburg PA
CBHW071032050326
40689CB00014B/3615